THOUGHTS OF PERFECTION

The I Attract Affirmations

EBRAHIM MONGRATIE

DEDICATION

May this book help you find your own self-worth,
Self-acceptance, true love for yourself and positive
possibilities.

CONTENTS

The information contained in this book is intended for general information purposes only and does not represent medical, legal or other professional advice on any subject matter. The information should not replace professional health care diagnosis, prescriptions or treat any diseases, condition, illness or injury. If you have or suspect that you have a medical problem, please contact your healthcare professional. The author is not responsible for misuse of the material found in this book.

INTRODUCTION

A few years ago I found myself completely broken by a traumatic experience which turned my life upside down. I was left with two choices on how I could move forward: spend the rest of my life with this pain or find a way to heal myself. My journey to love, peace, and joy was not easy for me, but eventually I found it. This book is a starting point to begin sharing some of what helped me to eventually find peace. My journey began when I came across a Japanese concept called Kintsukuroi, which is a technique for repairing broken pottery with seams of gold. I was attracted to the concept of Kintsukuroi because I realized there was an important message behind the concept: they could choose to throw the broken pottery away or find a way to put the pieces back together. I soon realized the parallels of this concept with my life; the broken pieces of my being could be put back together, all I needed was the determination to make it happen. Inspired by Kintsukuroi, I began the healing journey and in time I healed the emotional pain I endured. I began to feel an unbelievable and pleasant sense of peace. My entire body began filling up with an overwhelming sensation of positive energy.

Despite the emotional trauma I had experienced, I focused on the belief that I have been extremely blessed and highly favored along the road called life. No matter what life throws at me, I will continue to believe that I am blessed and love every moment I experience.

My vision is simple: if you want something, attract it, take action to get it, and it will be yours.

My mission is to show you an extremely simple and easy way to achieve instant positivity and how to maintain this attitude.

My commitment is to offer you my experience in terms of attracting positive emotions. You deserve nothing but the best of what life has to offer. Reflected in my vision is my passion for something that works every time i.e. attracting positive emotions. My writing is about experiences which have taught me that good things come from having positive thoughts. I have coached people and witnessed a complete transformation in their lives.

When you attract a positive emotion and take steps towards achieving the emotion, God (The Universe) works in mysterious ways to help you. I have titled the book "Thoughts of Perfection" to emphasize how important your thoughts are. I must point out that perfection may be exceptionally challenging to achieve, however if you strive for it you will achieve excellence and a wonderful sense of achievement.

We live in two worlds, the inner world, which is comprised of your thoughts and feelings, and the outer world, which is the physical world where you use your positive thoughts and turn them into positive actions. Thoughts control your mood, thinking about something good will make you feel good.

Likewise, thinking about something bad will make you feel bad. Once you feel good, it will be easier to get things done.

The answer to your happiness and success is in your thoughts and your ability to get things done. Think about it: when somebody upsets you and you get angry, you naturally begin to think bad things. Things like "how could he do that?" Or "why did he do that?" Your mind begins to think negative thoughts which ultimately leads to negative feelings.

The best possible thing you can do is forgive the person or just accept people for who they are. This allows you to be at peace with yourself and move on. Granted, that the concept is much easier said than done.

However, once you have read this book and practiced some of the techniques, you will discover happiness and begin to think positively and radiate that positivity onto others.

I Attract thoughts of Perfection and make a concerted effort to always take positive actions.

THE I ATTRACT AFFIRMATIONS

"I ATTRACT happiness into my life."

THE I ATTRACT AFFIRMATIONS

The emotional pain I endured was unbearable. I could hardly breathe; every thought I had, was about my pain. The traumatic experience kept playing over and over in my head. I remember thinking why? Why me? Little did I realize that I was hurting myself even more by taking this kind of approach to life?

One day I saw a bumper sticker that read "Happiness will come to you when you are happy". I did not comprehend what I had read and wondered how happiness could only come to me when I am happy? I went home and reflected on those words, I was determined to make sense of it in order to attain happiness.

I then came to the conclusion that although I am not happy right now, I can surely attract happiness. What happened next was amazing.

I said the following out loud: "I attract happiness into my life" and suddenly I began to feel a tad better. As I said the words out loud I felt the strength of these words travel through my body, I made sure that every part of my body felt the power of happiness. I continued repeating the words, the more I said the more I believed it and the belief came from adding the step of allowing my body to feel the power of the word happiness. "I Attract happiness into my life" even though the pain was there, saying these words out loud and feeling the power of the words in my body seemed to ease the pain. Furthermore, it gave me the courage to take action towards healing the pain.

If you want to experience a positive emotion, you must attract it. And to attract it, you must say the word associated with the emotion. An example of this is love, the more you say the word love the more you feel love. Repeating the word generates a positive feeling in your body.

Think about a person that constantly lies, eventually they begin to believe their own lies. The same applies to affirmations the more you say it, the more your brain registers it as a fact.

"I am feeling **good** today". The more you say it, the more you begin to believe it. Allowing your body to feel the power of the word "**good**" helps you to believe in what you are saying. Using the combination of words and feeling makes it easier to constantly feel good. Affirmations are positive statements that describe an end result you desire.

Negative words are never used in affirmations; you should eliminate negative words or a negative outcome from your thoughts.

When an affirmation is used correctly it becomes a great tool for achieving success and for improving your life. However an affirmation without a corresponding action is a job half done. I believe using the right affirmations attract corresponding events and situations into your life. It also helps you focus your mind on your goals and in turn it positively changes your habits, behavior and attitude.

Apply the following when repeating an affirmation:

Be relaxed as you can.

Pay complete attention to the words you are repeating.

Have faith in what you are saying.

Most importantly, make sure you allow yourself to feel the power of the affirmation in your body. E.g. in the happiness affirmation I connected to the feeling of happiness.

To enhance the affirmation process, use the following technique. Focus all of your attention onto your heart and breathe in through your nose while saying the following in your mind "I attract happiness into my life" and then breathe out while saying the following in your mind "I attract happiness into my life" Do this at least 5 times, I found this technique to be most effective when using affirmations. Remember to use this breathing

technique while using the other affirmations in the book.

Remember, with this affirmation exercise you will be saying and repeating what you want to be true in your life. If you apply the above steps when beginning your affirmation, you should see and feel, both mentally and emotionally, that it is true, regardless of your current situation.

If you have prepared yourself following the above directions, your mind is now ready. All that's left to do is take the action required to finally achieve what you desire. This affirmation exercise will give you the positive attitude, which will make it easier to take the required action.

Only some individuals take the action needed to succeed; if all you are looking for is happiness, then you should be able to achieve the feeling after simply saying the affirmation. However, if you want success you need to take the next step which is to allow yourself to feel the power of happiness and then take action towards attaining more happiness.

Once you begin to feel happiness you should feel inner peace among yourself. With this new-found happiness, the next step is to apply this to the world around you and do things to maintain the happiness.

On my personal journey, the following steps worked wonders for me:

I wrote about my emotional pain and how it affected me. Writing about my feelings felt far more effective than talking to someone about it. You are able to be completely honest and don't feel like you have anything to hide. Try it yourself and see if you can feel the difference.

I began to show gratitude for all that I have in my life. Expressing gratitude makes you feel happier, more optimistic about the future, and can help you feel physically healthier.

I performed random acts of kindness. I donated money to my favorite charity, I volunteered at a senior home, I planted a tree, I visited animal shelters, I allowed people to cut in front of me in traffic (without feeling angry), and I donate old clothes and old books. All of these actions allowed me to give back to the world and made me feel good knowing I was helping others.

I began motivating others. Much like performing random acts of kindness, I found this to be a sure way of maintaining my happiness.

I spend money on experiences instead of material things. I eat out, I go to concerts, I go to a theatre, I go on holidays (and go as often as I can), I tried paintballing, and I tried going carting, bungee jumping, and sky diving.

IMPROVEMENT...

"I ATTRACT the ability to improve every aspect of my life"

IMPROVEMENT

T he next step of my journey towards "Thoughts of perfection" was recognizing that in order to be open to improving myself, 1 needed to learn new things. I realized if I was not open to constructive feedback, I could not improve my life. Improvement is now an ongoing goal of mine. This book is all about improvement; how adopting a different way of thinking can help you take progressive action! The book is a beginner's guide which is made up of easy to use affirmations and tools to help you on the journey of life. Before implementing the suggestions, I recommend you read the entire book and then focus on one topic per day. Using this method of focus will help you achieve better results.

This life change all begins with improvement. All I want you to be thinking about today is how you can create a better you!

Before you begin the improvement journey, I want you to try to live in the present; not the future and not the past. This is the present and the start of an awesome life ahead of you. I want you to enjoy this beautiful moment: look around and take note of what is around you and feel the power of the present moment. Think about nothing but the moment you are in currently.

Forget about any complaints that you may have. Forget about your pain. Look around and just enjoy this moment. You are always going to remember this, for it is the moment when your life will begin to change for the better. I want you to let go, be bold, and expect the best for yourself.

We begin with the improvement affirmation:

"I attract the ability to improve every aspect of my life"

Take a deep breath and say it again with conviction.

"I attract the ability to improve every aspect of my life".

One more time!

"I attract the ability to improve every aspect of my life"

There you go. You may need to repeat the affirmation a few more times until you begin to believe it.

From now on, be willing to do the unthinkable and be open to doing things a bit different. Always follow your heart and do what feels right for you.

Here are a few things I did, and continue to do, that helped me dramatically improve my life.

I began to care for people around me.

I share and focus on what I can do for others.

I always try to be honest.

I work on being honorable and respectable.

I believe in integrity.

I follow my passion, no matter what people have to say.

I focus on my strengths.

I am authentic, and always myself.

I realized that it is okay to lose arguments.

I practice courage.

I surround myself with positive people.

I experiment.

I dream.

I began learning a new language

I practice self-discipline.

I travel as much as I can.

I began to enjoy nature.

I hug trees and benefit from the amazing energy trees radiate.

I relax more.

I drink lots of water.

I take the stairs.

I tried Yoga and Pilates and love it.

I go for a massage at least once or twice a month.

I meditate.

I am always grateful.

I forgive and I respect others.

I pray.

"I ATTRACT the ability to improve every aspect of my life"

CHANGE...

"I ATTRACT the capacity to change for the better."

CHANGE

Looking back on my life I can honestly say I detested change. I never appreciated the fact that I was in a constant state of change; I sat back and hoped all the bad will simply go away if I ignored it. It never did.

People always told me to face my fears. I never actually realized the true meaning and the power of this saying until now. The fact is, great things will happen when you have the courage to face your fears and embrace change.

Change is inevitable; therefore embrace it by firstly getting rid of all your painful memories and bad habits. I have a technique in the form of visualization I believe can help you get rid of past burdens and bad memories. I will share this technique with you in the next section but first, I would like to share something which truly amazed me and gave me the enthusiasm to make changes in my life: The rebirth of an Eagle, I came across this amazing story on YouTube, go check it out. It is a fictional story of how an Eagle goes through a 150 day change process. Although the details about the Eagle are fictitious, the message of change is profound.

Your journey should begin by changing your perspective and focusing on the positives of every situation. Change must always begin with you, not your environment and not with the need to change others. Most of us would like to change the World for the better, this can only happen by making sure you live your life with calmness, peace, gratitude and respect. Once you can do this, make sure you teach it to your immediate family; let them see you live this way as people learn from actions not by what you tell them. Radiate this kind of approach to life everywhere you go.

Say the following affirmation, sincerely and with belief. "I attract the capacity to change for the better." Say it a few times and then start your amazing change process by making an effort to change.

Be willing to work hard.

Don't expect overnight success or change.

Get out of your comfort zone.

Always live in the present moment.

Learn something new.

Take a different route to work.

Get up early and exercise.

As you can see, change requires you to take action. Stand up and make it happen. Always see change as exciting and empowering; always believe that you adapt to change with absolute ease. Most importantly though, believe that through change you are creating a happier life for yourself.

"I ATTRACT the capacity to change for the better."

VISUALIZE IT...

"I ATTRACT the ability to visualize my dreams."

VISUALIZE IT

In the previous section I mentioned that in order to change, you need to get rid of old memories and bad habits; I found a way to do this through visualization. The technique is extremely powerful and worked wonders for me.

Practice visualization on your own when you have at least 10 minutes to spare.

To begin your visualization, lie down on your bed during a quiet time (day or night). Then try to remember a moment in your life that caused you excessive emotional pain or disappointment. This may be incredibly difficult for you; however, like I mentioned before, facing your fears will help you grow.

Let's say you have pain from your childhood. This is what you need to do to dissolve the pain. While lying down, close your eyes and count from 10 to 0. When you get to zero I want you to visualize yourself in the moment after you experienced emotional trauma. Now imagine the adult you stepping into the moment and seeing the younger you dealing with this pain. Imagine yourself going towards the younger you and saying, "Hi, I am here, it is me (say your name) the older you. I have come from the future to tell you that everything is going to be okay. What you are feeling now will pass. I love you and will always be with you. I love you and nobody is ever going to hurt you again. No matter what, I will always be by your side. I love you."

Mention that you grew up to be a successful happy person. Saying I love you is extremely important, say it as much as possible to the younger you. Keep on reassuring your love and that everything is going to be okay and you will always be there.

This is just an example. You can say anything you want to the younger you as long as they are encouraging, positive words. Finally, wave goodbye and say: "please remember I am with you all the time. Whenever you need me, I will be here. Things work out perfectly for us."

When you open your eyes from this exercise, you will begin to feel better, happier, and at peace. Repeat this a few more times on other days and then move on to the next painful moment you experienced.

An additional form of visualization that worked for me was the ability to visualize what I want and what I need to do. All you have to do is imagine the end result, the moment when all your hard work has paid off. Don't think about how you are going to get there, just imagine yourself doing what it is at the end. If your goal is to win a marathon, imagine yourself on the podium holding your gold medal. Imagine how you going to feel: your smile, the atmosphere, people cheering, and all the good things that accompany winning. Use visualization as   part of your training not your only training.

Visualization is incredibly powerful; it can help you accomplish anything. When you visualize something, your subconscious doesn't know it is only in your imagination. It watches the event taking place in your thoughts and accepts that it is actually happening in that moment.

Visualization only works when you are calm and able to give yourself time to focus in absolute peace, free from your daily worries. Relax, stay calm, and start by living in the present moment.

Look around you and take in the detail of the environment. Look and listen, you will be amazed at how calm this will make you feel.

Let's say you want to go Bungee jumping but you are too afraid to do it. Visualization can help you take the jump. Visualize yourself just about to take the jump: you are tied up and ready to go. Imagine yourself looking down, feel the adrenaline rushing through your body. You lift your hands, count down from 3 to 0 and then you jump. Visualize the moment and what it may feel like. Run through the visualization a few times, immediately before the jump. This is the starting point of actually taking the jump. Now, take the next step and jump!

Listed below are four of the major benefits of visualization:

1.   It sparks your creative subconscious.

2.   It programs your brain in a positive way.

3.   It serves to activate the law of attraction.

4.   It increases your internal motivation.

I want you to pick out the one thing you have always wanted to do and then start visualizing yourself doing it.

The next and most significant step is the part that involves action; visualization alone will not get you to your goal. You need a "just do it" attitude. Visualize the end result and then work towards getting there; take action and do the unthinkable.

Begin today; do not wait.

Another surprisingly useful technique is the utilization of a vision board. Create pictures of your goals and pin them to your vision board. Place the board where you can view it every day. Whenever you visit the board, imagine the pictures are already a part of your reality.

Take steps to reach your goal, and remember that looking at the picture every day only serves as a reminder of your goal; you are still required to make it happen.

Remember, repetitive visualization and the willingness to take the necessary steps to get you there will help you achieve your goals much easier.

"I ATTRACT the ability to visualize my dream."

OPEN MIND, OPEN HEART...

"I ATTRACT the beauty of an open mind and an open heart."

OPEN MIND, OPEN HEART

At times, when people experience emotional pain they build a wall around their heart and mind. I built this wall thinking I was protecting myself. For a while, I kept the bad things out but little did I know I was keeping out the good things, too. Fortunately, I recognized my mistakes when I began my change journey. Today I am all about readiness; anything is possible now that I have an open mind and an open heart.

The following is what I did to achieve this amazing state.

I use to think too much. My mind was constantly working and I needed to slow down. I tried many different techniques to stop over thinking but the only technique that worked was using my senses to slow down my mind. I learnt this in a Philosophy class. Try the following:

Sit down on a chair keeping your back straight, relax your hands by keeping them to the side and then slowly lift your hands and place them on your knees. Close your eyes and use your sense of touch by moving one of your toes, then move all your toes up and down. Next use your sense of smell by breathing in deeply through your nose; do this a few more times. Then use your sense of taste, move your tongue around and taste for whatever flavor may still be in your mouth. Now use your sense of sight by slowly opening your eyes and taking in all the color around you. Close your eyes again and use your sense of hearing, listen to the sounds around you, then listen to the sounds furthest away from you. Breathe in deeply and open your eyes. You should be feeling relaxed with a silent mind.

The next thing I did was try to listen to people, truly listen and every day I listened more. This helped me have an open mind. Everybody is lovable and I love everyone equally. I don't judge or discriminate. I have finally learnt to accept and love people for who they are; "it is not about me"

Try having an open mind by making an effort to learn something new today.

Spend five to ten minutes at work in a totally different department; ask questions about what they do.

Go online and watch a TED Talk, or a YouTube lecture on something totally out of your normal interests.

Talk to somebody at work or school you normally don't talk to, find out more about them and what they do.

Explore another culture or religion and for lunch have something to eat from that culture.

Blindfold yourself for a while and test your senses.

Play a game of chess or learn how to play a game of chess if you do not know how.

When it comes to my heart, I have learned to love this amazing organ in my body.

I speak to my heart and the amazing energy I receive in return is incredible. Try it: put your hand on your heart and say "I love my heart and my heart loves me". Move your hand around your heart and repeat the words as much as you like. Enjoy the amazing feeling you getting from this moment.

The benefits of having an open heart are:

You will have room for growth, forgiveness and change.

You will be comfortable with learning something new.

Your heart will know how to heal and forgive.

You will not be afraid to love deeply.

You will be patient and wise.

You will be filled with positivity.

All of these thoughts are possible and achievable; it all starts with having an open mind and then taking the required action to make things happen. Without action nothing will change.

I ATTRACT the beauty of an open mind and an open heart.

HONEST WITH YOURSELF...

"I ATTRACT the ability to be honest with myself."

HONEST WITH YOURSELF

I was forced to be honest with myself, as I wanted to change my life and focus on a world without all the pain. At this point, I was already on the journey to a better life; however, I needed to answer some questions. Questions I had never asked myself before; other people probably did but I was deep into my own self-pity to take notice.

The questions were:

Do you mind being wrong or do you always want to be right?

Are you spending time increasing your talent or increasing your character?

Do you have the courage to take full responsibility for everything you think, feel, and do without blaming others?

How much effort are you willing to put into improving your life?

What do you love doing?

Reflect upon these questions and remember you made a choice to embark on the journey towards "thoughts of perfection", to change the way you think and feel. The affirmation that follows is a crucial step in that direction.

I want you to reflect upon the questions above immediately after you say the following affirmation: "I attract the ability to be honest with myself". Repeat the affirmation a few times.

Once you start feeling you can be honest with yourself, write down the answers to the questions above. Remember today is about being honest with yourself. Once you have answered the questions I have posed above, I want you to sit in a quiet place, clear your mind, and tell yourself "This is who I am. I acknowledge who I am. I love who I am. I attract the ability to be honest with myself and I will use my honesty to better myself. My honesty is my success."

Being honest with yourself will soon resonate to every aspect of your life. People will start to identify this wonderful quality in you. People will begin to see you as more reliable and balanced.

Now say this again, "I attract the ability to be honest with myself. My honesty is my success".

Now for the action plan:

Set aside some time for yourself where you can sit and think. I prefer to take a walk and think but you can do what works for you.

Take a moment to evaluate your life and write down things you are good at and decide on things you can improve upon. Write down all the things you would like to do in the next five to ten years, a bucket list if you like.

Now, commit to making improvements and doing everything you have registered on your bucket list.

Keep a log and tick off everything you manage to do.

It is your life and you are responsible for your own destiny, go make it happen.

WHAT COULD GO RIGHT?

"I ATTRACT the ability to think about what could go right."

WHAT COULD GO RIGHT

I attract the ability to think about what could go right. I use this affirmation instead of constantly worrying about what could go wrong, because I learned the power of thinking about what could go right.

Follow these steps to make your lifestyle change.

Today is 'no worry' day. You are going to stop worrying about everything that could go wrong and instead think about what could go right.

Changing your thought pattern to what could go right is an amazingly powerful ability, which I believe could change your life.

It is human nature to worry about things that could go wrong; we analyze, think, think, and think about everything that could go wrong.

More often than not, the things we worry about eventually happen, exactly as we worried about them.

Now try the reverse, think about what could go right. Once you make the decision to change your thoughts to think about what could go right, you will find an immediate change in how you feel. Ask yourself these questions:

What are the pros?

What are the positives?

What could go right?

Imagine a positive outcome and focus only on that, for that is where your success lies.

Remember; never think about what could go wrong.

I am not saying everything in your life is going to go perfectly well, what I am saying is making decisions will no longer be filled with worry and the fear of disappointment. You will begin to feel positive; happiness will find you and generally everything will work out perfectly for you, as long as you think about what could go right and then take the steps towards making sure everything does just that.

"I ATTRACT the ability to think about what could go right."

BELIEVE IN YOURSELF...

"I ATTRACT the ability to believe in myself."

BELIEVE IN YOURSELF

Once I learnt to believe in myself, everything fell into place. I am now able to fill my entire body with belief, I feel it rush through my body – I believe, I believe, I believe, I believe that I can do anything.

Today, everything will begin to fall into place for you. Begin your day by telling yourself the following:

I am amazing.

I am outstanding.

I am stunning.

I am breath taking.

I am awesome.

I am sensational.

I am remarkable.

I am spectacular.

I am incredible.

I am wonderful.

I am loveable.

I can do anything I set my mind to!

Now say the affirmation, "I attract the ability to believe in myself". Follow this affirmation with all of the "I am" qualities listed above.

Before you go to sleep tonight, just before you dose off, repeat everything above.

Positive thoughts right before you sleep at night will stick in your mind and can easily become your reality. Believing in yourself is one of the keys to your success.

Everything I have asked you to do above is important for you. You will begin to re-program your mind to believe in yourself.

You were born believing in yourself and as the years passed, you began to stop believing. Perhaps it was listening to the negativity of others, or allowing people to tell you what you can or cannot do.

If you still finding it difficult to believe in yourself, here are some tips to help you realize how awesome you are.

Identify the skills you have, you probably have many and are not conscious of them. To find out what they are, simply look at what people compliment you about and identify the things you don't struggle with. Write all these things down.

Learn from your failures: your past failures are a source of your future successes. Failure is a learning opportunity, embrace it.

Stop listening to negative people. This is the most important point of all, negative people will bring you down and steal your energy. Always surround yourself with positive people who inspire you and bring out the best in you.

Love yourself: be kind to yourself by saying I love myself. Say it daily and as much as you can. Feel it, believe it.

Accept compliments: this is extremely important in your quest towards building your self-esteem. When you receive a compliment again, do not dismiss it or question its authenticity. Take it as a truth, believe, and embrace it. Yes, you are awesome!

The confidence of your belief in yourself will make the difference time and time again. You don't need intelligence, opportunity, or resources. All you need is to believe in yourself.

The next few pages are in the form of advice. I ask you to be open to the messages I wish to convey. Reflect upon each section as you may discover opportunities to lead you to happiness and success.

"I attract the ability to believe in myself."

ACCOUNTABILITY

...

*"I ATTRACT the ability to hold myself to the
highest degree of accountability."*

ACCOUNTABILITY

I attract the ability to hold myself to the highest degree of accountability. I found myself saying this a few times until I grasped the complete understanding of its meaning. To further understand this affirmation I needed to know what accountability means and the simplest explanation I could find was:

Accountability is the obligation of a person to account for his or her activities while accepting responsibility for them.

Make a decision and don't look back. If the decision you made was wrong, you must take accountability and not make excuses or try to justify your decision. If you hurt someone's feelings in the process, you must apologize. Say the affirmation again: "I attract the ability to hold myself to the highest degree of accountability"

Holding yourself accountable will increase your performance, resulting in the ability to achieve success. Your connection with others will improve and you will gain a growing number of people who will respect you. The best and most amazing part of holding yourself accountable is that your self-esteem will begin to improve dramatically. It is nobody else's job but yours to make sure you are doing the things you know you should be doing.

Here are some examples of where you need to be keeping yourself accountable.

5.   The way you communicate with others should always be done with respect.

6.   Be accountable with your time.

7.   Your behavior and manners.

8.   You're eating habits and exercise routine.

9.   Your attitude and thoughts.

10.   The way you respond to challenges.

11.   Your punctuality.

12.   Your cleanliness.

13.   Spending less money than you earn.

14. Completing your to do list.

15. Your goals and finally your relationships.

Most importantly, you can choose your thoughts, keep yourself accountable for your thoughts and work towards "thoughts of perfection".

"I ATTRACT the ability to hold myself to the highest degree of accountability."

CONQUER...

"I ATTRACT the wisdom to conquer myself."

CONQUER

The fact you have made it to this point of the book means that you want to conquer yourself and reach your goals. At this point, you need to realize you are responsible for your own destiny. Everything begins with you including your attitude and self-discipline, as well as the belief that you can conquer yourself before you conquer the world. The affirmation to help you believe this is: "I attract the wisdom to conquer myself". Say the affirmation and believe it... "I attract the wisdom to conquer myself".

Now it's time to get out of your comfort zone; step out and take the risk because if you don't, you won't be learning and growing. Some of us learn from our mistakes and others learn from our successes. Appreciate both your failures and successes; however, your failures are where your current wisdom was formed.

Take this moment to express your gratitude and say to yourself, "I appreciate my past failures and I have learned from them".

The 3 important steps to conquering yourself are:

Boost your confidence level – this will help you meet new challenges.

Become more passionate about the things you desire, this will make you unobstructed by temptations and distractions.

Believe you have the ability to do anything – say the words out loud, "I can do anything".

Once you believe you can do anything, you will easily be able to work through any obstacle you face.

"I attract the wisdom to conquer myself."

ANGER...

"I ATTRACT the genius to release suppressed anger."

ANGER

Anger is something we all struggle with, though the consequences of being angry can sometimes be disastrous. Anger is nothing more than a deeper feeling of fear, hurt, disappointment, and pain. Managing anger can be a huge advantage in life. I recommend taking control of your anger before it takes control over you.

First off, you need to get rid of the pain and disappointment from your past. You can do this by using my visualization technique I shared with you in the visualization section. Some people store their anger by suppressing it, which can be dangerous. Use the following affirmation to help yourself with overcoming your anger, "I attract the genius to release suppressed anger". Say this affirmation until you believe it and can feel the anger flowing away. The next time you become angry about something, touch your fingertips on your left hand to the fingertips on your right hand and imagine yourself releasing the anger downwards, feel it simmer and disperse inside. Breathe in deeply. It is extremely important to make sure you breathe in deeply from your core; this will help relax you much quicker.

I attract the genius to release suppressed anger.

Another bad emotion that brings forth the same danger of anger is hatred. Hatred is a powerful emotion, which could end up killing you. Why do you want to hang on to this crazy emotion, which does nothing to the person it is aimed at? The subject of your hatred may be merrily going on with their life, while you continue to harbor dangerous emotions, causing you nothing but unpleasant thoughts.

Remember you are aiming for the thought of perfection, if you do hate something or somebody, now is the time to release them from your emotions. I have no doubt something bad happened, causing you to feel this way; somebody must have hurt your feelings or worse. At this time, I need you to focus on yourself.

First, despite what happened to you, please know you are an amazing, beautiful human being with an abundance of love to give. The hatred you feel is a choice you have made; it is time to make a new choice to free yourself from the hatred.

Now say this:

I am full of happiness. I am full of love. I am at peace with myself. I have the power to choose how I feel, and I choose to feel at peace.

Feel the hatred you were harboring leave your body, and in its place you will feel a great sense of freedom and peace. Now, take a deep breath and enjoy the present moment.

"I ATTRACT the ability to eliminate hatred from my heart."

LOVE YOURSELF...

"I ATTRACT the capability to love myself"

LOVE YOURSELF

Most of us spend our entire life in search of love; however, not everyone finds it. I found myself searching for love in all the wrong places until I discovered the love I have always been searching for, inside of me.

You must truly love yourself before you can love another. Although I recommend you always put your love for God first. To assist with this, let's begin with the affirmation "I attract the capability to love myself". Although you may not believe it, it is not difficult to love yourself.

You are an amazing person and the love you seek exists inside of you. Now it is time to unlock it with the affirmation, "I attract the capability to love myself". Once you find the power to love yourself, great things will happen to you. In addition, once you love yourself, it becomes easier for others to love you back. This is all part of the journey to the thoughts of perfection.

Please do not turn the page until you can tell yourself that you love yourself, and truly mean it. Feel it; touch your heart and say it, "I love myself".

Speak from your heart and say it again, "I love myself".

You are now part of an incredible moment and I want you to take a minute to enjoy it; I want you to breathe it in, feel the joy of the moment. Keep your hand on your heart and feel the love from within you rush through your body.

In this moment, you have probably felt more alive than you ever have before; this is the power of finding love within yourself. I want you to see yourself as a beautiful, radiant being filled with love.

If you finding it difficult to love yourself, here are a few things to work on:

16.   Celebrate your past

17.   Let go of your previous mistakes

18.   Never compare yourself to anyone else

19.   Live in the moment

20.   Sing your own praises

21.   Appreciate your life

22.   Laugh, even at yourself

23.   Smile more

24.   Brace yourself for an amazing future

"I ATTRACT the capability to love myself"

HEAL YOURSELF...

"I ATTRACT the power to heal myself"

HEAL YOURSELF

Y ou have the power within you to heal yourself. Today, I will share with you how to unlock this phenomenal ability. You have healing energies within your body; you can control the power of these energies if you believe in them.

Before we get into the affirmation and the healing process, I would like you to begin a cleansing process. Eliminate all harmful things you put into your body. Eat properly, stop smoking, get more sleep, and exercise regularly. Over and above the body cleansing process practice everything you have read in the book thus far, then and only then, will you be able to connect with healing energies. Let's begin with the affirmation: "I attract the power to heal myself"

Here is an example of how to use these energies: Let's say you find yourself with a common cold. You are lying in bed feeling terrible and all you are thinking about is how sick you are feeling. Now, stop thinking about being sick. Say, "Healing energies are flowing through my body". (*Remember to breathe in and think about the affirmation and breathe out while thinking*

about the affirmation, do this between 10 and 20 times)
Now, when you say it, I want you to connect with these healing energies; feel them flowing through your body. Start with the healing energies in your head and begin to control the movement of the healing energies, down to the rest of your body. Begin to bring the healing energies back up your body, or anywhere you want the healing energies to go. Finally, say "I am feeling great" and smile. Go through this process a few times, if necessary. When you are done, smile at yourself and take a shower; you going to feel much better after.

Getting better, both mentally and physically, is also all about your thoughts. You hear of people overcoming cancer, and yet you hear of people dying from cancer. Those who completely healed must have had positive thoughts and were determined to recover. Let me also say these positive energy techniques should not be used in isolation; use them alongside the treatment you are currently receiving from your doctor or physician.

Aside from everything else, you should listen to your body as well as your intuition. Nobody knows your body better than you; if you truly listen you will find the answer to what your body requires. Sometimes, all your body needs is a charge of energy; you can do this by using the tips of your fingers on both hands to brush your entire body for two minutes. Begin to brush your body from your head down. It is quite an amazing feeling, go on and try it.

Another form of healing I highly recommend is crystal healing. Crystals have unique internal structures that resonate at a certain frequency. The resonance gives the crystals the ability to heal and harmonize the mind, body, and soul; they also neutralize negativity and lift depression.

Rose Quartz crystals can be used for cleansing and detoxifying the emotions. Opal promotes emotional balance and stability. Amethyst works on hormone production, balancing emotional highs and lows and helping you to feel more in control. Amethyst also relieves stress by reducing mental burdens and helping you to focus on realistic goals. Amber can be used to neutralize a negative state of mind and balance any underlying emotional imbalance.

Black Tourmaline is for protection against negative energy of all kinds and is a grounding stone.

These are just a few of the many crystals available for healing. I recommend doing some research and going out and purchasing one that fits your needs; keep these crystals on you and in your home, whenever you need them.

Again please note, these techniques should not be used in isolation; use them alongside the treatment you are currently receiving from your doctor or physician.

Healing energies await you.

"I attract the power to heal myself"

PATIENCE...

"I ATTRACT the staying power of patience."

PATIENCE

Most of my life I struggled with having patience; I wanted what I wanted instantly. All I heard was people saying 'have patience' or 'be patient' but they never told me how to be patient or how to maintain the patience.

Over the years I managed to train myself to be patient? It took me a while to realize that success comes from being patient. Patience is enduring; it will test you over and over until you submit to being patient. The following affirmation will help you make a start to being patient, "I attract the staying power of patience".

Remember, for an affirmation to work effectively you must say it as much as possible in order for your brain to see it as a fact. I suggest you start by saying this affirmations five times, "I attract the staying power of patience". Repeat this affirmation another five times. Now, put it into practice and use it as a strategy to achieve your goals. Patience will help solve problems more easily, one step at a time. Live in the moment and focus on the present of any situation.

When you find yourself in long queues (i.e. waiting for a bus or plane) and you become impatient, use the time to say the patience affirmation: "I attract the endurance of patience" and then use the time to visualize your goals.

Here are a few things to keep in mind:

25.   When you have a huge task ahead of you, visualize a positive result and then take it one step at a time and appreciate what you have accomplished at each step.

2.   When things are getting too intense, go for a walk to clear your head. While you are walking, enjoy the present moment and all of your surroundings. Look at something like a flower, leaf, or tree and enjoy its beauty.

3.   Try the trusted method of counting to 10 before you speak in a heated situation. This will give you time to remember what truly matters to you.

4.   Smile! When you are feeling stressed, force yourself to smile. 10 seconds is all it takes. Stop and take a deep breath and just smile. You will be amazed at how amazing you are going to feel after you do this.

5.   Ask for help, you cannot always do everything yourself.

"I ATTRACT the staying power of patience."

BLISS...

"I ATTRACT a state of perpetual bliss."

BLISS

Let me define bliss: Bliss is an emotional state described as peace or happiness. I am absolutely sure you want to achieve bliss, if you know the feeling, try remembering a moment of bliss, keep it in your mind and say, "I attract a state of perpetual bliss".

Bliss is extremely powerful, when you in a state of bliss, you begin to radiate positive energy which brings you more bliss. Now, find your bliss. It is as simple as finding the one or many things that make you extremely happy. Today, I want you to identify your bliss and just do it, do your blissful act but don't stop; do it every day and you will soon discover many other blissful opportunities.

You can find your bliss by:

26.   Being open to new ideas and opportunities.

3.   Being curious, ask questions and try new things; you may just like it.

5.	Be willing to let go; you are free to do anything you want to do. Don't let the worry of what others may think stop you.

6.	Be willing to step outside of your comfort zone, for outside of this is where you will find wonderful things.

Trust life and what it brings forth; you may just find yourself in a situation you never thought you would ever be in and through that experience, you may just find bliss.

Now, find your bliss at work. Bliss and work do not need to be separated. Find what you love doing and make it your job. It's not going to happen overnight but take small steps to finding bliss at work. Once you decide to follow your bliss, all good things will be yours for the taking.

"I ATTRACT a state of perpetual bliss."

FEAR...

"I ATTRACT the power to overcome the fear of failure."

FEAR

We all struggle with fear, making it an important emotion we often must overcome.

Are you afraid to fail?

Do you always play it safe?

Do you worry about making mistakes?

Are you always looking for other people's approval?

Do you lack confidence in your abilities?

It is time to master the ability of overcoming the fear of failure. We begin with an affirmation because belief is the first step in overcoming the fear of failure: "**I attract the ability to overcome the fear of failure.**"

Make the right choice. Fear is merely an emotion you choose to feel, let it go. Before we get back to the affirmation, here are a few things you need to do:

27.   Identify your bad habits and try to eliminate them.

28.   Learn to find success in your failures.

29.   Learn from those who have succeeded; confidently use their formulas for success.

30.   Pursue what makes you happy and success will find you.

Back to the affirmation: "I attract the power to overcome the fear of failure." Repeat it another 20 times.

Each time you say this affirmation, I want you to feel the fear slipping away. The more you say the affirmation, the more fearless you will actually become. You will start to feel empowered, allowing you to rise above your fears.

Your fear is now becoming weaker... "I attract the power to overcome the fear of failure." Your fears are becoming insignificant... "I attract the power to overcome the fear of failure."

You will feel even more strengthened and empowered..."I attract the power to overcome the fear of failure."

You will no longer experience the fear...

You can now rise above the fear of failure and take a bold step towards making whatever you want into a reality. You can do it.

"I attract the power to overcome the fear of failure."

FORGIVENESS...

"I ATTRACT the wisdom of

forgiveness."

FORGIVENESS

Today is going to be an incredible day, A WOW day. You will go to sleep tonight feeling content and completely at peace. Let's begin....

You are presented with the wonderful opportunity to forgive somebody today. It is time to let go.... But first let us master the affirmation: "**I attract the wisdom of forgiveness**."

This affirmation refers without a doubt to peace. When you hold pain in your heart, you are the loser, and when you hold on to a grudge against someone, you are the one who loses, not them. You carry the pain, not them, and why do that to yourself? Say this affirmation a few more times: "I attract the wisdom of forgiveness."

Things to remember when you are ready to forgive:

> 31. Forgiveness is for you, not for anyone else.

> 32. Forgive and you will find peace. You do not necessarily have to reconcile a friendship with the person or condone that person's actions.

4.   Never expect the person to apologize before you forgive; forgiveness primarily concerns itself with your inner peace.

Forgiveness reduces:

Anger

Hurt

Depression

Stress

Now, choose to forgive and feel the pain leave your body.

Call the person or send them an email expressing your forgiveness.

WOW! Peace is certainly yours. Well done. Your heart is ready to give and receive love...

You are now one step closer to thoughts of perfection.

"I attract the wisdom of forgiveness."

BEING THANKFUL...

"I ATTRACT the ability to be thankful for all I have in my life."

BEING THANKFUL

Be thankful for everything in your life. Now, keep in mind that you have to be sincere about this. Imagine your boss only gives you a 1% annual increase this year. Your first instinct may certainly be "@#$$# how did this happen? I deserve more than this for all my hard work!" Well, that reaction is certainly not the most appropriate or desirable. The correct reaction should be "WOW, thank you. I am blessed to first and foremost have a job, and furthermore, this 1% will surely go a long way." Mean it, and be thankful.

I firmly believe that being thankful for something like this will increase opportunities and possibilities in your life, similarly being ungrateful will close doors of opportunity for you. When I was much younger I frequently visited a friend of mine and occasionally his parents invited me to stay for Dinner. The pre-Dinner experience was amazing, each person had to say thank you for everything they experienced in their day. Each person also thanked as many people as possible from their teachers to the lady serving lunch at School to their friends and bus driver, basically anybody that had an impact on their day.

It was allot of fun but only later in life did I realize the significance of this amazing act of gratitude. I now say thank you as often as I can.

Even if things don't work out for you, say thank you for the experience you gained.

I was once in an amazing relationship that didn't work out and at times I would reminisce and feel sad that the relationship ended, however the moment I said thank you for the time I got to spend with her, I found peace.

Begin your gratitude journey by saying the following affirmation: "I ATTRACT the ability to be thankful for all I have in my life."

Say thank you as much as you can each day of your life, even if you only say it to yourself.

Thank you, thank you, thank you...

"I ATTRACT the ability to be thankful for all I have in my life."

LISTEN...

"I ATTRACT the ability to listen."

LISTEN

Listen to people and give them your full attention. Never stop listening and never interrupt; just listen, listen, and listen more. This is without a doubt the most important skill you will need in your personal and professional life.

Once you can truly listen with empathy, people will instantly like you and find ways to help you get what you want.

Here are some simple tips to help you develop this skill:

First, believe that you already possess this skill and then perform the following steps:

Give your full attention to the person who is speaking.

Make sure your mind is focused in the moment and on the person.

Always keep an open mind.

Let the person finish talking before you start speaking.

Once the person is done speaking, ask questions. Doing this will help you better understand what the person is trying to tell to you. Try summarizing everything you have heard. Give feedback while keeping eye contact with the person. Don't forget to use the affirmation "I attract the ability to listen."

Today, spend the rest of your day by listening more and talking less. You just might hear something amazing.

TALK TO THE
HEART OF OTHERS...

*"I ATTRACT the ability
to talk to the hearts of others."*

TALK TO THE HEART
OF OTHERS

We begin with the affirmation: "I attract the ability to talk to the hearts of others."

Before you repeat the affirmation, let's first explore the importance and relevance of this affirmation with regards to thoughts of perfection. We are all connected in some strange way, and that connection is something you control. I believe in creating a peaceful connection, a connection of love, peace, and joy. I want to be able to bring out the best in people instead of the worst. I close my eyes at night knowing that each day I have connected with people and that through the connection, I have transferred positive energy. In that moment, I brought some form of joy to another person. I spoke to their heart. Today, you are going to connect with others and speak to their hearts.

Now, it is time to repeat the affirmation "I attract the ability to talk to the hearts of others." Say it again and believe it.

"I attract the ability to talk to the hearts of others."

Try to connect to the first human you see today. When you pass a stranger smile and say good morning, and feel yourself saying good morning from your heart to theirs.

When you see somebody you know do the same thing, and don't forget eye contact! Shake the persons hand and ask how they are.

The hand shake will allow you to transfer some positive energy and, when you do shake the person's hand, I want you to feel like you're transferring some positive energy from your heart. Feel the energy being transferred from your heart though your arm, and out of your hand into theirs. Compliment the person by saying something nice like, "You're looking good today."

If you're a manager or have your own small business try to do this with each of your employees every day. If you have too many, try to reach as many as possible. When you have those busy, stressful days take some time out to go speak to your employees, starting with the handshake. You will find that taking time out to chat to people like this recharges you, and when you give others your positive energy you actually receive double back

Talking to the heart of others is not difficult at all, people just want you to show sincerity in how you interact with them.

"I ATTRACT the ability to talk to the hearts of others."

HELPING OTHERS...

"I ATTRACT the ability to help others."

HELPING OTHERS

I attract the ability to help others. I believe that helping others is one of the main reasons we are put on this earth. It's all too easy to forget about others, with our hectic schedules and technological focus.

Your challenge today is to make a difference in someone's life. Simple things can go a long way, keep a look out for someone that needs help. Say the affirmation as much as you can and watch how quickly you will get to help someone. I want you to think success, not for you, but for somebody else. Find a way to help somebody succeed and their success will be your success.

Remember that life is not just about you. The person you help will be eternally grateful and will possibly be saying good prayers for you, and we all need good prayers.

Ask yourself, who can I help? Reach the person and find a way to help them succeed. Your success depends on it.

Still not sure how to go about helping others? Try this:

Ask someone what you can help with. Try a colleague, friend, or family member. You won't believe what good can come out of this.

Listen to someone, and through this you will find a way to help them. Even if listening is all they needed someone to do.

Find something to help with in your community, volunteer at a soup kitchen or a shelter, or simply donate some money to an important cause.

Stop and help. If you see someone on the street struggling to carry bags, offer to lighten their load.

Don't expect reward or praise in return. What matters is that you were able to help somebody.

"I attract the ability to help others."

POSITIVE POSSIBILITIES...

"I ATTRACT positive possibilities into my life."

POSITIVE POSSIBILITIES

When you wake up in the morning your thoughts are in your control, and you have the ability right there and then to choose how the rest of your day goes. You simply make a choice to attract positive possibilities for the rest of the day. If you wake up feeling sad or depressed, you need to firstly acknowledge the feelings and then tell yourself, "I can choose how I feel," or "I can do this."

Remember one of my previous affirmations: "I attract happiness into my life". Use it, and make the rest of your day about attracting positive possibilities. When you're having a stressful day and you bump into somebody you know and they ask you how your day is, 9 times of out of 10 you're going to say, "I am having a bad day." This would be the incorrect answer.

Even though you're telling this to somebody else, your mind is going to register this as a fact and the rest of your day will continue to be bad. See, you are attracting more stress. Instead say, "I am having a wonderful day." Then say the affirmation "I attract positive possibilities into my life."

The rest of your day will be about attracting positive possibilities.

Some of the benefits of always believing in positive possibilities are:

33.   Your mind will always stay motivated because you are only focused on a positive outcome.

34.   As you create feelings of excitement about a positive future, you have more happiness and enjoyment as well as peace of mind.

35.   The belief helps you align your life to positive outcomes and, as such, increase your chance of success.

36.   Focusing on positive possibilities helps eliminate negative thoughts.

Remember, believe in what you say and say it as often as you can. One more affirmation... "I attract the ability to focus on positive possibilities."

"I ATTRACT positive possibilities into my life."

POSITIVE
PEOPLE...

"I ATTRACT positive people into my life."

POSITIVE PEOPLE

This is an important one, positive people. What kind of people do you attract? With this affirmation you are going to attract positive people. "I attract positive people into my life".

Now, if you are already surrounded by negative people in your life and they just happen to be family or people that you cannot possibly walk away from, fear not. Here is how you deal with them, and deal with them you must because if you don't you will become just like them. Negative people never seem to see the positive side of anything until somebody points it out to them. Your job is to listen, and then continuously point out the positives. This will be noticeably difficult for you in the beginning, but don't give up.

Eventually they are going to see the light, or they may just stop speaking to you about their negative thoughts.

If you're positive, you're naturally going to attract positive people. The next few pages will guide you on how to be more positive. Meanwhile, focus on the people you are associating with, and start working on limiting your engagement with negative people or start pointing out positivity to them.

Then seek out more positive people. Associating with positive people makes you feel better about yourself and your ability to achieve your goals. Their positivity will rub off on you, and make things easier for you to rub the same positivity onto others.

Here are a few things to do to attract positive people into your life:

> 37.   Identify your positive traits and project them to the world.

> 38.   Let love flow through you and onto everybody else.

> 39.   Use meditation to increase your happiness. This will help you radiate positivity.

> 40.   Continually work on healing your dark side.

> 41.   Let yourself be found by putting yourself out there. Introduce yourself to people, and be friendly.

As you can see, attracting positive people into your life is a process that will take time and commitment.

It all starts with being more positive yourself.

"I ATTRACT positive people into my life."

POSITIVITY...

"I ATTRACT positivity into my life."

POSITIVITY

Only good things come from being positive.
I'm sure you have heard this often. Go ahead and attract more positivity into your life, and then radiate that positivity onto others? That way positivity comes back to you in many ways. It is an awesome feeling and all you have to do is attract positivity into your life. Say the following affirmation and believe in it: "I attract positivity into my life." Say it as much as you can all day today.

Some benefits of positivity include:

42.   The ability to easily bounce back from setbacks.

5.   Being able to connect with positive people.

6.   Effortlessly achieving your goals by being astonishingly creative.

7.   Coping better with stress.

5.   It is good for your health.

Once you embrace positivity it becomes incredibly addictive and when you are faced with a setback, you naturally find the positivity in the situation. You will easily be able to change your thoughts to positive thoughts. "I attract positivity into my life." Believing in this brings more and more positivity and success into your life, and soon you will only expect great things to happen in your life. Every new day will be the best day of your life if you seek out joy, play as often as you can, and find adventure.

Once you find positivity, share it. Sharing and helping others to be more positive helps with your own sustainable positivity. Radiate positivity whenever you can, and share the love. It is going to make you feel awesome and at the same time you will be changing the world one step at a time.

Positivity and negativity is contagious, which of these energies would you much rather be spreading?

I ATTRACT a positive future...

I ATTRACT positivity into my life...

I ATTRACT the power to radiate positivity onto others...

EXERCISE...

"I ATTRACT the energy and enthusiasm to exercise daily."

EXERCISE

Maintaining a healthy body will certainly help develop a healthy mind, which is what you need to strive for. If you're not already exercising daily, then this affirmation is for you. Attract the energy, the time, and the enthusiasm to exercise. Start using the following affirmation: "I attract the energy and enthusiasm to exercise daily." Now, say it a few times.

Remember To enhance the affirmation process by focusing all of your attention onto your heart and breathe in through your nose while saying the following in your mind "I ATTRACT the energy and enthusiasm to exercise daily" and then breathe out while saying the following in your mind "I ATTRACT the energy and enthusiasm to exercise daily" repetition is key.

You can also say the affirmation to energize yourself when you have time to exercise but find that you don't have the energy or willpower to do it. "I attract the energy and enthusiasm to exercise daily."

For now, forget about weight loss; exercise simply because it makes you feel good!

The other benefits of exercising are endless, but here are just a few of them:

43.   It strengthens your immune system, helping your body prevent disease.

44.   It can improve mental health.

45.   It prevents depression.

46.   It also helps build positive self-esteem.

47.   It helps to increase your sex drive.

You don't necessarily have to join a gym to exercise. All you have to do is establish a routine and stick to it.

Find a bodybuilding website, on these websites, you will find workout routines and 6 to 12 week programs that will get you into shape and feeling great. If you don't want anything hectic, simply start by walking for 20 minutes per day. Today, smartphones allow you to download an application that can keep track of your steps. Download one and set up a steps-per-day goal. Make sure to meet your goal every day.

I highly recommend yoga as a form of exercise. The benefits of yoga include:

6.   Improved flexibility.

7.   It helps build muscle.

8.   It promotes good posture.

9.   It prevents degenerative arthritis.

10.   It helps keep your spinal disks fit.

11.   It strengthens bones and assists with warding off osteoporosis.

12.   Yoga also assists with lowering blood sugar.

These are just a few of the benefits of yoga. I would advise attending yoga classes, but if you don't have time or money for that, then I suggest you go to a yoga website and find a few routines you can do at home. I have also seen some awesome yoga applications for most smartphones out there.

"I ATTRACT the energy and enthusiasm to exercise daily."

CALM

I ATTRACT the ability to take a calmer more relaxed approach to life.

CALM

I attract the ability to take a calmer more relaxed approach to life. This affirmation commands me to slow down; the idea of a calmer relaxed approach to life seems absolutely heavenly.

I am aware that calmness is a choice I make; I can choose to live my life with calmness, peace and gratitude. I can choose to relax whenever I want to. All I need is the ability to train myself to make these choices when needed.

The calmness I seek is a state of serenity, tranquility and peace. When I said the affirmation a few times, I began to think about prayer. Prayer brings me a sense of peace, therefore my calmness conquest began with prayer. I pray as much as I can, even if I am praying for the well-being of others.

When I put my hands together and pray it is as if God has calmed my heart.

I suddenly feel quietness and calmness around me. I am instantly silenced by the beauty that surrounds me in the moment of prayer; I am reminded that God is without a doubt most gracious and most merciful.

I also found that simply getting away from it all and spending more time in nature increases my state of calmness. I love being around trees, I pay attention to the movement of the trees, it has a calming effect on me. My mind relaxes and I feel peaceful and grounded. Perhaps it's all to do with the breathable air trees provide.

In 2004, Japan's National Land Afforestation promotion organization conducted an experiment and found that a walk in the forest had beneficial effects on blood pressure, heart rate and immune system. They also found that people who just looked at a forest view for 20 minutes had a 13 per cent lower concentration of the stress hormone cortisol.

A few other things that I am certain will contribute to a calmer life are:

> 48.   Read more, reading is a great way to relax and is proven to lead to better overall sleep.

> 49.   Smile more, even for no reason at all.

> 50.   Take more naps, a short nap is a significant benefit for improved alertness and performance.

> 51.   Get a pet, Cats and Dogs in particular can reduce stress, anxiety and depression. They ease loneliness, encourage exercise and even improve your cardiovascular health.

52.   Drink more water. When the body is dehydrated it can induce anxiety, nervousness and stress.

53.   Take an occasional break from technology, like smartphones. This can help reduce anxiety, depression, stress and fatigue. It can increase your personal wellness, help with relationships and increase your overall happiness.

54.   Connect more with family and friends. People with solid family or social networks are generally healthier.

55.   Give more hugs; this helps your body release Oxytocin which is beneficial in reducing fear and anxiety.

56.   Enjoy food by eating slowly. Not only will you have more time to enjoy the taste of your food but you may also be losing weight and reducing digestive problems, this all leads to stress free healthy living.

57. Live in the moment, this is true freedom which makes you more grateful and appreciative.

58. Appreciate the things you have and say thank you as often as you can, even to yourself.

I attract the ability to take a calmer more relaxed approach to life.

SMILE...

"I ATTRACT the healing power of

smiling."

SMILE

T he best form of charity is to smile at someone, yet many people find it difficult to do this pleasantly simple act. "I attract the healing power of smiling." Today you are going to smile as much as you can. Smile while driving to work, smile at a stranger, and, in fact, smile at everybody you walk past, and I do mean everybody. Smiling has many other benefits:

People will trust you more quickly. Smiling is contagious, and it's something you want to spread. Studies have shown that people who smile more live longer. If you're a single women looking for a man, smile and they will come to you. Smiling makes you look beautiful. If you count calories then smiling is perfect for you, as smiling helps you burn calories.

If you are someone that struggles with smiling, try the following tips:

59. Practice in front of a mirror to get used to the feeling.

60. Think of happy thoughts or think of someone you love.

61. Observe other people smiling. Remember, it is contagious.

62. Fake a smile until it becomes real.

Smiling makes you feel good and will make others feel good too. It's the easiest way to bring joy to the world. Go ahead and start making a difference in the world one smile at a time.

Try it now: smile! You look good doing it!

STAND OUT IN A CROWD...

"I ATTRACT the readiness to stand out in a crowd."

STAND OUT IN A CROWD

B e proud of who you are. Why worry about what people think of you? When you were a baby, you often stood out in a crowd, either with your cute smile or by crying for your mother's attention. As the years went by, you began to tell yourself stories: "If I do this, people will think that, if I do that people will think this." The truth is people will have an opinion no matter what you do. Choose to live freely and be in the moment. If the moment requires you to stand out, then stand out.

Start your day by using the following affirmation: "**I attract the readiness to stand out in a crowd**."

If you are afraid of standing out, then I suggest you say this affirmation at least 15 times. Every time you say it, you will begin to notice that the fear is gradually fading away.

Control your breathing (breathe deeply) and continue saying the affirmation. Remember that the more you say this affirmation, the more your brain begins to accept it as fact.

To stand out, practice the following tips:

> 63. Be able to think for yourself. Don't always adopt the thought processes of everyone else. You need to think outside the box.

> 13. Never allow yourself to be swayed by others; if you believe in something, you must demonstrate that you have confidence in what you saying.

> 7. Always be willing to take risks and never be afraid of failure.

> 8. Remember to practice good manners and to always be polite. Shake people's hands and smile.

> 6. Be willing to show initiative.

> 6. Dress for success.

If you dedicate your time to practicing these suggestions, you will soon be the life of the party, and you won't worry about what people are thinking of you. Life is just more fun when you choose to let go of fearing other people's opinions.

"I attract the readiness to stand out in a crowd.

PERSEVERANCE TO WIN...

"I ATTRACT the patience and perseverance to win."

PERSEVERANCE TO WIN

Today is about taking stock of all your goals.

The truth about goals is that you have to live and breathe them every day in order to actually achieve them. The key is having the patience and perseverance to see them through. We begin with the affirmation: "I attract the patience and perseverance to win."

Life will throw all kinds of hurdles your way, and people will be people and not see or understand your vision. No matter what, don't give up on anything; believe in yourself and in what you want to achieve.

Remember to:

64.   Get rid of all self-doubt. You can do this.

14.   Always stay cool. Dedicate your energy only to your goals and not on irrelevant trivialities.

8.   Never listen to others who say you cannot do it, because you can and you will.

9.   Learn from your mistakes as you go through the process of achieving your goals.

7.   Keep your mind and body healthy.

7.   Stay true to who you are and never let anyone or any situation change who you are.

7.   If you feel mental or physical pain, you have to find a way to overcome it. Never quit.

NEVER QUIT...

All day today: "I attract the patience and perseverance to win." This affirmation is an extremely important one, and it is an affirmation that you should say every day. By now, you ought to realize that achieving your goals ultimately requires hard work. This affirmation will strengthen your commitment to achieving those goals.

You were born to win; persevere, and the win will be yours.

"I ATTRACT the patience and perseverance to win."

POSSIBILITIES WITHOUT LIMITATIONS...

"I ATTRACT the ability to see possibilities without limitation."

POSSIBILITIES WITHOUT LIMITATIONS

In one of the previous sections we covered positive possibilities, and now we affirm new possibilities. "I attract the ability to see possibilities without limitation." This affirmation is extremely powerful. "I attract the ability to see possibilities without limitation."

You create your own destiny, and it begins with the way in which you imagine your future to be. The key to all possibility lies within you and you alone. Don't defeat yourself by holding on to the belief that you are not good enough or smart enough; you can conquer this way of thinking by believing that you can accomplish anything.

Begin with the following:

> 65.   Let go of everything holding you back. What's holding you back? NOTHING – it is only your fear of failure. Let go of it.

66.   Be willing to put in the necessary effort and energy and to take the steps required to shift your belief.

67.   Fortify your courage; the courage you need to move beyond what you previously thought was not possible.

68.   Maintain the belief that everything will without a doubt work out perfectly.

69.   Eliminate negativity from your life.

Do you remember the visualization affirmation? "I attract the ability to visualize my dream." Use it in conjunction with this affirmation.

Think of something you want and visualize yourself attaining it….Now that you know how you would feel if you were to get what you want, focus on the goal and remember, **no limitations**. You will get there, and you will get what you want; all you have to do is believe and see the possibility with no limitations.

I simply cannot emphasize the importance of seeing possibilities without limitations enough. It is the starting point of any dream. No limitations, no limitations, no limitations, no limitations, no limitations. Now, say this:

I will get what I want.

I am going to get what I want.

I believe in no limitations.

Remember that once you become aware of your possibility, write it down and focus on it every day.

It will be yours.

> *"I attract the ability to see possibilities without limitation."*

PRAYER...

"I ATTRACT the healing and relieving power of prayer."

PRAYER

Prayer involves maintaining closeness with the source of all that is good; it is healing and relieving.

The simple act of merely extending your hands in prayer brings an instant feeling of calmness and a sense of peace within your being. Try it. Put your hands out like a beggar and pray. Pray for whatever your heart desires and pray continually….

Your attitude during prayer is extremely important. Always be humble and keep your mind focused and free from negative thoughts.

When I pray I ground myself and connect to the Earth, I visualize myself and the entire planet entwined and submitting to GOD. In this moment my heart is instantly calmed. The moment is full of beauty, calmness and love.

The moment after prayer is always a perfect time to be grateful for all I have in my life and for that reason I spend a minute saying thank you, thank you, thank you. I say thank you for as much as I can.

Remember that prayer is not a guarantee against pain and suffering and that what you ask for may not be given to you immediately. In fact, you may never receive what you ask for because perhaps it doesn't align with the plans of God, who knows what is truly best for you. Nevertheless, never ever stop praying and remember to always make a good prayer for somebody else as well.

ABUNDANCE...

"I ATTRACT unlimited abundance into my life."

ABUNDANCE

Abundance is an extremely large quantity of something. I would like you to consider abundance as a large quantity of everything wonderful for you:

An abundance of love

An abundance of joy

An abundance of friends

An abundance of positivity

Make your own abundance list and start attracting all the abundance you need. Whatever your current circumstances are, you can choose to feel abundant. You don't need a huge bank account or a fancy car; simply choosing to feel abundance is free.

You should always feel as though you have the best of everything. You are abundantly joyful.

An absolutely important practice to adopt before starting your abundance journey is to be thankful for everything in your life. Say the words "Thank you" and say them as often as you can. If you are not thankful for everything you already have in your life, then it is very likely you blocking out an abundance of better things.

Attract an abundance of positivity and know that everything you need will come into your life at its appointed time.

ACCEPTANCE...

"I ATTRACT the ability to accept others without judgment or criticism."

ACCEPTANCE

Acceptance is a choice, and once you make that choice and move forward in your life, you will find peace. Let me explain. Imagine that you find yourself in a situation that you cannot change no matter how hard you try, like being in love with someone who does not love you back, for example. You will try and win them over and you will also experience stress because of this situation.

However, there comes a time when you have to move on, and once you accept the fact that you have to move on, you will find peace. You will begin to feel happy, and if you continue to accept the situation, you will go from merely feeling happy to actually being happy.

Along the road called life, you are going to meet all sorts of people. Some of them you will like instantly and some of them will grow on you. Then you will find the people you are going to try to change. Trying to change people will always result in a failure on your part. You must accept people for who they are, because this acceptance is the key to you being happy when you are around them.

Never let circumstances change who you are. If you stay true to whom you are and accept people for who they are, they will soon embrace your acceptance of them. Once they do that, let your positivity radiate onto them. Your positivity will create a beautiful light that will captivate them and inspire them to want to be more like you.

Nothing is permanent and everything changes in time. Therefore, if you are going through a difficult time, accept that it is a difficult time in your life and then visualize a positive outcome.

Finally, take some form of positive action to make a difference in the current situation.

"I ATTRACT the ability to accept others without judgment or criticism."

ACTION...

"I ATTRACT the ability to take action towards achieving my goals."

ACTION

By now you should have mastered "Thoughts of Perfection" and how to maintain positive thoughts; the next huge step to your success is to develop the ability to take action and make things happen. Without taking this step, gaining the ability to achieve success will not be easy and may in fact never happen. A positive action taken today will create a wonderful tomorrow.

Most people know what action needs to be taken to change their lives. However, the problem lies in the fact that the action that must be taken is stuck in their head.

They think too much and repeat the terrible words "One day I will do that," and then what happens? One day never comes. Train yourself to never put off tasks for later. If something needs to be done, do it immediately.

No matter how small the task, complete it immediately.

Force yourself to be interested in the task, and spend a few minutes focusing on the first part of the task. This practice will help give you the desire to complete the task. Once you are in the habit of doing things right away, those big ideas in your head can easily be turned into action.

Say the affirmation and believe that you have the ability to take action.

"I ATTRACT the ability to take action towards achieving my goals."

Thoughts of perfection

Maintain thoughts of perfection by being thankful, exercising and praying every day.

.

Read a few pages of this book daily or return to it when you need some motivation, it will help you maintain positive energy.

Always be cognizant of the fact that you should seek to know yourself. Begin by attracting the ability to know yourself. "I attract the ability to know myself"

I have come to learn that everything I want is within me, the first time I realized this was when I discovered the love I have always been searching for is within me. I now love myself; this love brings me an overwhelming sensation of self-fulfillment.

I sustained the sensation by recognizing what makes me happy.

What makes me the utmost happiest is being able to help somebody. Making somebody smile, saying something nice to them, making them feel good by sharing positivity, and sharing whatever I have learnt over the years and if all the information is passed on it can multiply and multiply.

Thank you for reading my book, I hope I have inspired you in some way.

Believe in yourself.

ALL THE AFFIRMATIONS

*Reminder

Enhance the affirmation process by focusing all of your attention onto your heart and breathe in through your nose while saying the affirmation in your mind and then breathe out while saying the affirmation in your mind. Repetition is key

I attract happiness into my life.

I attract the ability to improve every aspect of my life.

I attract positive possibilities into my life.

I attract positive people into my life.

I attract positivity into my life.

I attract a positive future.

I attract the power to radiate positivity onto others.

I attract the ability to be thankful for all I have in my life.

I attract the energy and enthusiasm to exercise daily.

I attract the ability to take a calmer more relaxed approach to life.

I attract the ability to listen, listen, and listen.

I attract the capacity to change for the better.

I attract the genius to release suppressed anger.

I attract the joy of eliminating hatred from my heart.

I attract the healing power of smiling.

I attract the ability to help others.

I attract the beauty of an open mind and an open heart.

I attract the ability to be open with myself.

I attract the readiness to stand out in a crowd.

I attract the patience and perseverance to win.

I attract the wisdom of forgiveness.

I attract the ability to see possibilities without limitation.

I attract the ability to think about what could go right.

I attract the ability to believe in myself.

I attract the ability to visualize my dream.

I attract the ability to hold myself to the highest degree of accountability.

I attract the wisdom to conquer myself.

I attract the endurance of patience.

I attract the ability to talk to the heart of others.

I attract the ability to love myself.

I attract a state of perpetual bliss.

I attract the power to overcome the fear of failure.

I attract the power to heal myself.

I attract the healing and relieving power of prayer.

162

I attract unlimited abundance into my life.

I attract the ability to accept others without judgment or criticism.

I attract the ability to take action towards achieving my goals…

I attract the ability to know myself